TOP TORQUES

RACING CARS

ROB COLSON

WAYLAND

First published in 2016 by Wayland
Copyright © Wayland 2016

Wayland, an imprint of
Hachette Children's Group
Part of Hodder & Stoughton
Carmelite House
50 Victoria Embankment
London EC4Y 0DZ

Editor: Elizabeth Brent

Produced for Wayland by
Tall Tree Ltd
Designed by Jonathan Vipond

ISBN 978 0 7502 9766 0
Library eBook ISBN 978 0 7502 9477 5
Dewey number: 629.2'28-dc23

10 9 8 7 6 5 4 3 2 1

Printed in China

An Hachette UK company
www.hachette.co.uk
www.hachettechildrens.co.uk

Please note: the website addresses (URLs)
included in this book were valid at the time
of going to press. However, because of the
nature of the Internet, it is possible that
some addresses may have changed, or
sites may have changed or closed down
since publication. While the author and
publishers regret any inconvenience this
may cause to the readers, no responsibility
for any such changes can be accepted by
either the author or the publishers.

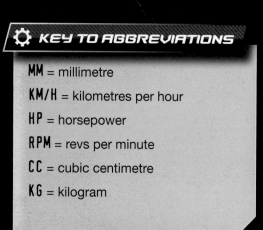

⚙ KEY TO ABBREVIATIONS

MM = millimetre

KM/H = kilometres per hour

HP = horsepower

RPM = revs per minute

CC = cubic centimetre

KG = kilogram

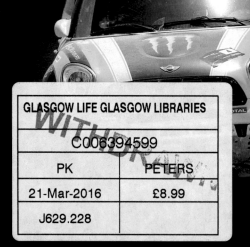

Words in bold appear in the glossary.

The publisher would like to thank the
following for their kind permission to
reproduce their photographs:

Key: (t) top; (c) centre; (b) bottom; (l) left;
(r) right

Front cover: David Acosta Allely/
Dreamstime.com, back cover: Manfred
Steinbach/Shutterstock.com, 1 Audi AG,
2 Rodrigo Garrido/Shutterstock.com,
3 General Motors, 4b Citroën Racing,
4–5 Mercedes AMG Petronas, 5t Audi AG,
5b Audi AG, 6–7 Herranderssvensson/Creative
Commons Sharealike, 6b Christian Delbert/
Dreamstime.com, 7t Library of Congress, 7c
ckirkman/Creative Commons Attribution, 7b
Art Konovalov/Shutterstock.com, 8, 8–9, 9
Mercedes AMG Petronas, 10–11 General
Motors, 10bl General Motors, 10br Hodag
Media/Shutterstock.com, 11b Action Sports
Photography/Shutterstock.com, 12–13, 13t,
13b General Motors, 14b Oskar Schuler/
Shutterstock.com, 14–15 Audi AG, 15
esbobeldijk/Shutterstock.com, 16 Rodrigo
Garrido/Shutterstock.com, 16–17 Alex Zarubi/
Dreamstime.com, 17b Rodrigo Garrido/
Shutterstock.com, 18–19, 19t Ford Motor
Company, 16c, 16b Rodrigo Garrido/
Shutterstock.com, 20, 20–21, 22 Citroën
Racing, 22, 23t, 23b FIA, 24, 24–25, 25
Volkswagen, 26, 26–27 Action Sports
Photography/Shutterstock.com, 27 Manfred
Steinbach/Shutterstock.com, 28t Miroslav
Zajíc/Corbis, 28–29 Audi AG, 28b Laurentiuz/
Dreamstime.com, 29t Maurice Volmeyer/
Shutterstock.com, 30 Audi AG,
31 Mercedes AMG Petronas

CONTENTS

WHAT IS A RACING CAR?

DRIVER SAFETY
At high speeds, drivers need to be well protected. They wear helmets and fireproof suits, and are safely strapped in to their seats.

ENGINE
Racing cars can be fitted with petrol engines, hybrid petrol and electric, or just electric motors. In an F1 car, the engine sits behind the driver.

TRANSMISSION
The engine is connected to the wheels via a **gearbox**. F1 cars are rear-wheel drive, which means that the engine only powers the rear wheels.

All kinds of cars can be raced, from ordinary road cars to the powerful machines that compete in endurance races. They all have in common a need for speed. Manufacturers constantly search for ways to save weight or increase power, while staying within the race organizers' strict rules. Here, we take apart a Formula 1 car.

The Citroën C-Elysée is a production car that competes in touring car races.

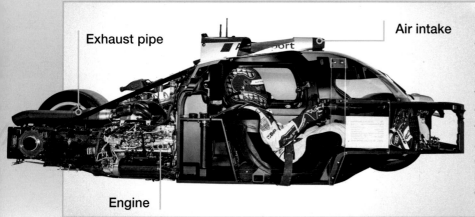

Exhaust pipe

Air intake

Engine

TIGHT FIT

This cutaway of an Audi R18 E-tron Quattro endurance car shows the car's distinctive driving position. The car sits low to the ground, which means that the driver has to lie almost horizontally. Seeing around the car from inside the cockpit can be a problem, so rear-view cameras show the drivers what is behind them.

CHASSIS

The **chassis** is the framework that gives a car its strength. It is made of lightweight but strong materials.

SUSPENSION

Suspension rods are attached to the wheels. The rods have springs attached. They give a smoother ride and better **handling** around corners.

BRAKES

The car is slowed by pushing brake pads against discs within the wheels.

WHEELS AND TYRES

The wheels in F1 cars are fitted with tyres that are much softer than the tyres on ordinary cars. The tyres have to be changed two or three times during a race.

AERODYNAMICS

Wings at the front and back of the car create downforce as air flows over them. This keeps the car safely gripping the road at high speeds or when taking corners.

OTHER RACE CARS

While Formula 1 cars are specially made for racing, the cars in many other forms of racing such as rallying are based on the production models you see on the road. The cars are heavily modified to add speed and safety. In endurance races, specially built cars called sports prototypes race alongside modified production cars.

The Audi R18 E-tron Quattro is a sports prototype.

THE HISTORY OF RACING CARS

The earliest car races took place on public roads in the late 19th century. By 1900, cars could reach speeds of 80 km/h, and concerns for safety led to a decline in road racing. The first race on a **speedway** track was held in England in 1906, and racing took on a new lease of life. New kinds of races, including endurance, stock cars and off-road rallies, were developed.

1938–1951

ALFA ROMEO

158

Formula 1 started in 1947. Its early years were dominated by the Alfa Romeo 158, which won 47 of the 54 Grand Prix it entered. Argentinian driver Juan Manuel Fangio won the 1950 Formula 1 championship in this car.

1954–1957

JAGUAR

TOP SPEED:
260 KM/H

D-TYPE

The Jaguar D-type won the Le Mans 24-hour endurance race three times in a row from 1955 to 1957. The car's revolutionary design took technology used to make jet airplanes to produce a stylish **aerodynamic** shape. A lightweight aluminium body made the car even lighter and faster.

ROUND THE WORLD RACE

On 12 February 1908, six cars lined up in New York for the start of the longest motor race ever. They drove across North America, then took a ship to East Asia and raced all the way to Paris, France. The drivers had to cope with muddy tracks and freezing conditions as they crossed the wilds of Siberia. Just three cars finished the epic 35,000-kilometre race. The winner reached Paris in 169 days.

TOP SPEED:

310 KM/H

1970

PLYMOUTH

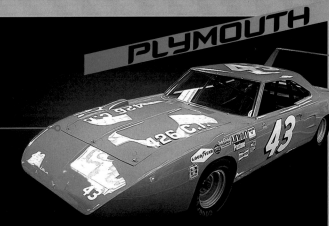

TOP SPEED:

230 KM/H

SUPERBIRD

The Superbird was a modified Plymouth Road Runner. It was made by the Chrysler company to race in the US NASCAR series. It was one of a series of fast racing cars nicknamed the 'aero warriors', which had aerodynamic noses and huge rear wings. Legendary driver Richard Petty drove a Superbird to eight victories in the 1970 NASCAR season.

TOP SPEED:

220 KM/H

1980–1991

AUDI

QUATTRO

The Audi Quattro was the most successful rally car of the early 1980s. In 1981, French driver Michèle Mouton won the Sanremo race in Italy driving an Audi Quattro. She was the first woman ever to win a world championship rally.

MERCEDES-BENZ

F1 W05 HYBRID

Formula 1 is the biggest motor racing competition of all. Each season, manufacturers have to come up with new cars. For 2014, they made cars powered by a petrol engine and an electric motor. The W05 was the best car of the year.

Rear suspension

Rear wing upper mainplane

REAR WHEELS: 510 x 240 MM

⚙ CUTTING EDGE

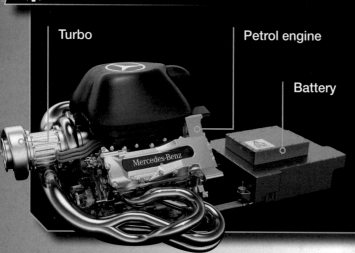

Turbo

Petrol engine

Battery

At the heart of the car's **power unit** is a small 1.6-litre petrol engine. A **turbocharger** recovers energy from the engine's **exhaust** fumes. Energy is also recovered from the car's brakes. This energy charges a battery, which powers the electric motor. The driver engages the motor to give an extra boost when accelerating.

TOP SPEED: **320** KM/H | 0–100 KM/H: **2.5** SECONDS

ENGINE: **1600** CC ⚡ WITH INTEGRATED ELECTRIC MOTOR

CYLINDERS: **V6**

GEARBOX: **8-SPEED**

TRANSMISSION: **REAR-WHEEL DRIVE**

A manual jack lifts the rear end.

Driver sits inside a central reinforced 'survival cell'.

New wheels are fitted.

Hydraulic jack at the front.

A central nut holds the new wheels in place.

Front suspension

PIT STOP

During each race, drivers come into the **pit lane** one or more times. The engineers jack the car up off the ground, replace the wheels and refuel the tank, then lower it back down to rejoin the race. The whole process takes less than 10 seconds. Teams practise pit stops for many hours – it can make the difference between winning and losing.

FRONT WHEELS: 510 x 215 MM

Front wing produces up to 40 per cent of the car's downforce.

MAXIMUM POWER: 750 HP (COMBINED)

SUSPENSION:	CHASSIS:	BRAKES:	FUEL CAPACITY:	WEIGHT:
CARBON-FIBRE WISHBONE	CARBON FIBRE	CERAMIC DISCS	RACE ALLOWANCE OF 100 KG	690 KG

DALLARA

DW12
INDYCAR

IndyCar is a series of races held on tracks around the USA. All the teams use the same Dallara chassis. Teams develop their own front and rear wings, but must then make these available to all the other teams. This makes for exciting, close races.

Front wing is made by the team.

PENSKE
Truck Rental

On wet tracks, the tyres need a deep tread to give extra grip.

FRONT WHEELS:
380 x 250 MM

FAST TYRES
In wet conditions, cars are fitted with tyres with a tread. In dry conditions, they use faster slick tyres. In addition, teams can choose an alternate tyre, marked with bright red sidewalls. These tyres are super fast around corners, but they are soft and wear out quickly, so using them is a risk.

TOP SPEED: 350 KM/H | 0-100 KM/H: 2.5 SECONDS

| ENGINE: 2200 CC | CYLINDERS: V6 | GEARBOX: 6-SPEED | TRANSMISSION: REAR-WHEEL DRIVE |

Driver sits in the middle of the car.

This IndyCar is powered by a Chevrolet engine.

The rear wheels are partly covered.

REAR WHEELS:
380 x 355 MM

CUTTING EDGE

IndyCar races take place on road courses or oval speedways. On oval tracks, the corners are banked to allow the cars to take them at high speeds. Cars are set up to only take left turns. The tyres lean to the right to balance the car on the banks. To the right of the driver's head is extra padding to protect against the force on the constant left turns.

MAXIMUM POWER: **700** HP

SUSPENSION:	BODY:	BRAKES:	FUEL CAPACITY:	WEIGHT:
DOUBLE PUSHROD	CARBON FIBRE	CARBON DISCS	70 LITRES	700 KG

CHEVROLET

SS NASCAR RACE CAR

The body has been modified to make it aerodynamic.

The NASCAR Sprint Cup is a competition for stock cars in the US. Stock cars are modified production cars. They are big and powerful, with great straight-line speed. The Chevrolet SS race car is based on the SS Sports Sedan production car.

FRONT WHEELS: 480 x 215 MM

A window net stops the driver from flying out of the car in a crash.

TOP SPEED: **320** KM/H | 0-100 KM/H: **4.7** SECONDS

ENGINE: **6200** CC

CYLINDERS: **V8**

GEARBOX: **4-SPEED**

TRANSMISSION: **REAR-WHEEL DRIVE**

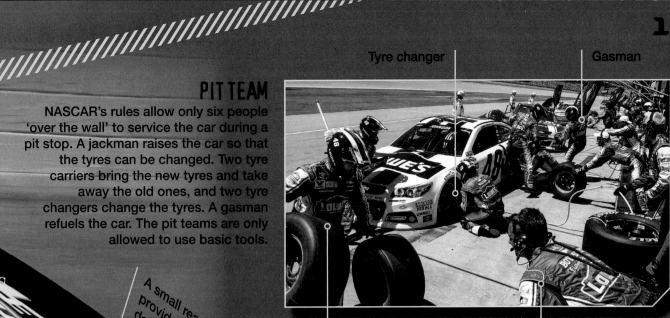

Tyre changer

Gasman

PIT TEAM

NASCAR's rules allow only six people 'over the wall' to service the car during a pit stop. A jackman raises the car so that the tyres can be changed. Two tyre carriers bring the new tyres and take away the old ones, and two tyre changers change the tyres. A gasman refuels the car. The pit teams are only allowed to use basic tools.

Tyre carrier

Team leader

A small rear wing provides extra downforce.

CUTTING EDGE

A head and neck restraint protects the driver from whiplash in the event of a crash.

Inside the cockpit of a stock car, everything but the essentials is stripped away. The controls are quite basic, and the driver changes gear using a manual gear stick. The driver is strapped into a safety seat, and the car is fitted with a fire extinguisher.

REAR WHEELS: 480 x 215 MM

MAXIMUM POWER: 415 HP

SUSPENSION: PUSHRODS

BODY: ALUMINIUM

BRAKES: VENTILATED DISCS

FUEL CAPACITY: 66 LITRES

WEIGHT 1540 KG

AUDI

R18 E-TRON QUATTRO

The R18 is an endurance car, designed to take part in long track races. This model competed at the Le Mans 24-hour race for the first time in 2014, finishing first and second. A diesel engine powers the rear wheels, while an electric motor provides extra power to drive the front wheels.

FRONT WHEELS:
460 x 375 mm

CUTTING EDGE

The rear wing generates lots of downforce when the car is travelling at high speeds.

There are two exhaust pipes at the rear of the car.

The car's strength is provided by its outer skin, or **monocoque**, which is a single piece of moulded **carbon fibre**, a material that is lightweight but strong. The monocoque is further strengthened by layers of fabric. The fabric makes it harder for sharp objects to pierce the monocoque in the case of an accident.

TOP SPEED: **300** KM/H | 0–100 KM/H: **3.2** SECONDS

ENGINE:
3700 CC WITH ELECTRIC MOTOR

CYLINDERS:
V6

GEARBOX:
7-SPEED

TRANSMISSION:
ALL-WHEEL DRIVE

The cockpit has to be wide to meet race rules.

REAR WHEELS:
460 x 370 mm

Wing mirrors sit over front wheels.

The lights use LEDs at low beam, but switch to lasers when the full beam is activated.

Air intake at the centre provides ventilation for the driver.

SMART LIGHTS

During long endurance races, drivers need to race right through the night. The R18's headlights are linked to satellites and programmed for each track. This allows them to anticipate a corner and point to the right place before the driver even turns the steering wheel.

MAXIMUM POWER (COMBINED): 490 HP

SUSPENSION:	CHASSIS:	BRAKES:	FUEL CAPACITY:	WEIGHT:
DOUBLE WISHBONE	CARBON FIBRE	CARBON CERAMIC DISCS	54 LITRES	870 KG

BMW

MINI ALL4 RACING

This modified Mini Countryman competes in cross country rallies. The rallies are raced over rough land, and take place in stages run over several days. The whole race may be up to 3,000 km long. Cars need to be extra-tough to last the course.

Body panels are easily removed to carry out maintenance on the road.

A sump guard protects the front of the car when it hits obstacles on the road.

TOUGH FRAME

The rally car is very different from an ordinary Mini. It is built around a tough steel tubular frame, which protects the driver. This is covered with carbon-fibre body panels. The rear doors are fake. From the original car, only the windscreen, door handles and lights remain.

A long suspension is needed to provide clearance over rocky terrain.

TOP SPEED: **178** KM/H | 0–100 KM/H: **6** SECONDS

ENGINE: **2993** CC | CYLINDERS: **6** | GEARBOX: **6-SPEED** | TRANSMISSION: ALL-WHEEL DRIVE

Spare tyres behind the driver.

CUTTING EDGE

The car has a huge 360-litre fuel tank at the rear. This is to ensure that there is enough fuel to cover at least 800 km. Some rallies cross remote deserts, so it is crucial that cars do not run out of petrol. They also carry three spare tyres.

TYRES: 245MM

MAXIMUM POWER: 311 HP

SUSPENSION:	BODY:	BRAKES:	FUEL CAPACITY:	WEIGHT:
STEEL SPRINGS	CARBON FIBRE	AIR-COOLED DISCS	360 LITRES	1900 KG

FORD
FIESTA RS WRC

The Fiesta RS WRC competes in the World Rally Championship (WRC). The car is based on the production Fiesta RS, but with added features for extra speed and safety.

Each stage of a rally takes place on a different course. A co-driver sits next to the driver and tells the driver what is coming up next on the course.

Rear wing

FRONT AND REAR WHEELS:
460 X 200 MM

The body is reinforced to give it extra strength.

TOP SPEED: **260** KM/H | 0–100 KM/H: **5 SECONDS**

ENGINE:	CYLINDERS:		GEARBOX:		TRANSMISSION:	
1600 CC	4		6-SPEED		ALL-WHEEL DRIVE	

⚙ CUTTING EDGE

All the cars in the WRC are based on ordinary production cars. However, the interior of the cars looks nothing like a road car. The driver and co-driver are strapped in to racing seats, and all unnecessary parts have been stripped out to save weight. A roll cage protects the occupants if the car rolls over.

Five-point racing seat belt.

Roll cage is an essential safety feature.

On a dirt track, the car is fitted with smaller wheels. Tyres have a deep tread for extra grip.

DIFFERENT SURFACES

The car is set up differently depending on the surface the stage will be raced over. On a dirt track, the suspension is softened and raised. This gives better clearance over bumps. On roads, the suspension is hardened and lowered to give extra speed.

Front grille allows air over the engine.

On tarmac roads, larger wheels and slick tyres are used.

MAXIMUM POWER: 300 HP AT 6000 RPM

SUSPENSION: STRUTS WITH ADJUSTABLE DAMPERS

BODY: STEEL AND FIBREGLASS

BRAKES: VENTILATED DISCS

FUEL CAPACITY: 40 LITRES

WEIGHT: 1200 KG

CITROËN

C-ELYSÉE WTCC

The C-Elysée was the dominant car in the 2014 World Touring Car Championship (WTCC), winning 14 out of the 15 races. The WTCC is a series of track races for production cars. All the cars have 1.6-litre turbocharged engines and six-speed gearboxes.

Bonnet vents allow air to flow over the engine.

FRONT AND REAR WHEELS:
460 x 250 MM

DRIVING POSITION
The driver sits low down and well back inside the cabin. This helps to keep the car balanced, which improves **performance**. The driver's thighs, hips and torso are held tightly in place by the seat so that they are stable when taking corners.

The steering wheel is attached to a long steering column so that the driver can reach it from a mid-car driving position.

TOP SPEED: 250 KM/H | 0–100 KM/H: 5 SECONDS

ENGINE:	CYLINDERS:	GEARBOX:	TRANSMISSION:
1598 CC	4	6-SPEED	FRONT-WHEEL DRIVE

Race regulations mean that cars must have four doors.

9
S. Loeb

Rear wing

⚙ CUTTING EDGE

Citroën designers started with the standard road car's shell, then heavily modified it to make the racing version. The **front splitter**, side skirts and rear wing improve the car's aerodynamics, reducing drag and increasing downforce. This improves handling, and allows the car to take corners more quickly. The wheel arches are higher to make room for larger tyres.

Front splitter

Side skirts

MAXIMUM POWER: 380 HP

SUSPENSION: SPRINGS AND GAS-FILLED DAMPERS

BODY: STEEL AND CARBON FIBRE

BRAKES: STEEL DISCS

FUEL CAPACITY: 50 LITRES

WEIGHT: 1100 KG

SPARK-RENAULT

SRT 01E

The rear wing is made from lightweight carbon.

The driver sits in a protected 'survival cell'.

REAR WHEELS:
690 x 305 MM

The car's chassis was designed by the manufacturer Dallara.

FRONT WHEELS:
650 x 260 MM

The Spark-Renault is a new kind of racing car that is powered entirely by an electric motor. It was developed to race in the Formula E series, which started in 2014. The 'e-Prix' take place around city-centre tracks. These electric cars are much quieter than their Formula 1 cousins. Even at full speed, they make little more noise than a normal road car.

TOP SPEED: 225 KM/H | **0–100 KM/H: 3 SECONDS**

ENGINE:	CYLINDERS:	GEARBOX:		TRANSMISSION:
ELECTRIC MOTOR	NONE	5-SPEED		REAR-WHEEL DRIVE

CUTTING EDGE

The cars are all fitted with the same McLaren electric motor, which is powered by a huge 200kg battery. The battery does not last the full distance. The drivers must make a pit stop halfway through the race to change to a fully charged car.

The motor sits behind the driver.

The same tyres are used in both dry and wet conditions.

Screen displays information from the race marshals.

Power controls

Paddle to change gear.

CONTROLS

The drivers can operate the car's controls without ever taking their hands off the steering wheel. There are paddles for changing gear and operating the **clutch**. The driver can talk to the pit lane via radio, while a screen displays information about the race.

MAXIMUM POWER: 270 HP

SUSPENSION:	CHASSIS:	BRAKES:	FUEL CAPACITY:	WEIGHT:
DOUBLE WISHBONES	CARBON FIBRE AND ALUMINIUM	METAL OR CERAMIC DISCS	N/A	888 KG

VOLKSWAGEN

POLO RX SUPERCAR

Large rear wing creates downforce even when sliding sideways.

Rallycross (RX) is an all-action form of car racing, in which production cars compete over mixed-surface tracks in short sprint races lasting under three minutes. The Polo RX Supercar is a powerful RX car capable of explosive acceleration around tight tracks.

REAR WHEELS:
430 x 205 MM

THRILLS AND SPILLS

In each round, five or six cars compete against one another. Races are close and collisions are commonplace. Each car must complete one 'joker' lap per race, where they take an alternative route for one lap. Drivers need to judge when to use their joker lap carefully – it can be the ideal time to overtake a rival without colliding.

TOP SPEED: **190** KM/H | 0–100 KM/H: **2.1** SECONDS

ENGINE: **1998** CC | CYLINDERS: **4** | GEARBOX: **6-SPEED** | TRANSMISSION: **ALL-WHEEL DRIVE**

CUTTING EDGE

To provide sure handling on the rough tracks, the car's engine always powers all four wheels. A part called a differential in the centre of the car allows the wheels to rotate at different speeds while they remain connected to the engine.

The radiator has been moved to the rear of the car to protect it from flying debris and other cars.

The average speed around the 1,000-metre tracks is 100 km/h.

Powerful turbocharged engine sits under the bonnet.

FRONT WHEELS:
430 x 205 MM

MAXIMUM POWER: 560 HP AT 6250 RPM

SUSPENSION:
DOUBLE WISHBONE

BODY:
REINFORCED STEEL

BRAKES:
VENTILATED DISCS

FUEL TANK:
COMPETITION FUEL CELL

WEIGHT:
1300 KG

TOP FUEL DRAGSTER

The dragster is 10 metres long.

Drag races are short sprints in a straight line. The fastest dragsters of all are called Top Fuel cars. These custom-built speed machines cover the 300-metre track in under four seconds.

A long, thin chassis helps to keep car stable and running in a straight line under extreme acceleration.

Parachute

END OF THE RACE

The dragsters are travelling at more than 500 km/h when they cross the line. By now, the cars are so hot that many parts of the engine and the clutch have melted. The engines have to be rebuilt at the end of every run. The drivers release a pair of parachutes to safely slow the cars down to a stop.

TOP SPEED: 500 KM/H | 0–160 KM/H: 0.8 SECONDS

ENGINE: 5000 cc | **CYLINDERS:** V8 | **GEARBOX:** NONE | **TRANSMISSION:** REAR-WHEEL DRIVE

'Wheelie bar' stops the car's front end from raising up and flipping over.

Massive rear wing creates downforce.

Driver sits inside a strong cage for safety.

REAR TYRES: 910 MM DIAMETER

CUTTING EDGE

At the starting line, the driver spins the dragster's wheels really quickly. This causes a 'burnout', which heats the tyres to full race temperature. Then they engage full power and take off. At full throttle, the engine burns as much fuel as a large passenger jet. Don't stand too close. The noise will burst your eardrums!

Huge air intake captures lots of air to burn the fuel.

The engine burns a special fuel called nitromethane.

The 'smoke' in a burnout is in reality mostly water vapour.

MAXIMUM POWER: UP TO 8000 HP

| SUSPENSION: RIDGE-MOUNTED | BODY: CARBON FIBRE AND MAGNESIUM ALLOY | BRAKES: PARACHUTES AND CARBON FIBRE ROTORS | FUEL CAPACITY: 50 L USED PER RACE | WEIGHT: 1050 KG |

24 HOURS OF LE MANS

The 24 Hours of Le Mans is a race held each year at Le Mans in France. Cars race around a track for 24 hours, and the car that has completed the most laps at the end is the winner. Each car has a team of three drivers, who take turns behind the wheel.

Until the 1970s, drivers had to sprint to their cars at the start of the race. Today, they start behind the wheel.

FAST TRACK

The 13.6-kilometre track covers roads that are open to the public for the rest of the year. It is a very fast track, and drivers are racing at full throttle most of the way round. The highest speeds are achieved on the long Mulsanne Straight, where cars reach over 300 km/h. At the end of the straight, they must quickly slow down to 100 km/h, putting great stress on the cars' brakes.

Dunlop Curve
Tertre Rouge
Chicane
Ford Chicane
New maison Blanche
Porsche Curve
L'Arche Chicane
Mulsanne Straight
La Florandière Chicane
Indianapolis
Arnage
Mulsanne Kink
Mulsanne

The Sarthe Track has been used for every race since the first one in 1923. Each section has a name.

DIFFERENT CLASSES

At Le Mans, purpose-built sports prototype cars race alongside modified production cars called **grand tourers**, which are not quite as fast. Cars are divided into different classes depending on the kind of car and the make-up of the driving team. In addition to an overall winner, there is a winner within each class.

The Aston Martin Vantage V8 competes in the Grand Tourer (GT) classes at Le Mans.

TEAM EFFORT

The race is a test of driver skill and stamina, and also of the car's reliability. The race engineers waiting in the pit lane are crucial for a successful team. Through the race, they may need to replace worn-out parts, and they will need to do it quickly. A major mechanical failure will see a car out of contention. More than 50 cars start the race, but many break down before the end.

A Spyker C8 Spyder GT2R stops for a check-up during the 2005 24 Hours of Le Mans.

The overall winner is always a sports prototype such as this Audi. The winner of the race will have driven more than 5,000 kilometres at an average speed of 240 km/h.

GLOSSARY

Aerodynamic
Shaped to minimize a force called air resistance.

Carbon fibre
A strong but lightweight modern material.

Chassis
The frame or skeleton of a car to which the car's body and engine are attached.

Clutch
A mechanism that disengages a car's transmission. It is used to change gear.

Cubic centimetre (cc)
A unit of measurement used to describe engine size. There are 1,000 cubic centimetres in a litre.

Cylinder
A chamber in the engine inside which pistons pump up and down to produce power.

Driveshaft
A system of rods that connects the engine to the gearbox, or the gearbox to the wheels.

Exhaust
Waste gases produced by burning fuel in the engine. The exhaust fumes are pushed out of the car through exhaust pipes.

Front splitter
A bar at the front of a car that disrupts airflow to produce downforce, which keeps the car from rising off the road.

Gearbox
A system of cogs that transfers power from the engine to the wheels. Low gears give power for acceleration or driving uphill. High gears are used at faster speeds.

Grand tourer
A car built to drive long distances. Modified grand tourers compete in endurance races.

Handling
The way in which a car responds to the driver's actions.

Horsepower
A measure of the power produced by a vehicle's engine.

Hybrid
A car powered by both a petrol engine and an electric motor.

Hydraulic
Powered by a system of pipes containing pressurized liquid or gas.

Monocoque
An outer shell on a vehicle that supports the vehicle's weight.

Nitromethane
A special fuel used in Top Fuel drag racing. It contains oxygen, which helps it to burn very quickly inside the engine.

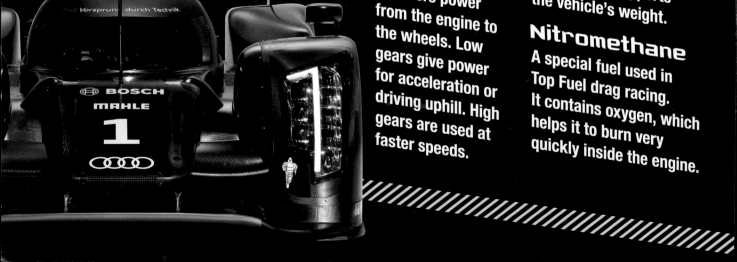

Performance

A measure of a car's handling. It includes top speed, acceleration and ease of taking corners.

Pit lane

A lane that runs parallel to the finishing straight on a race track. The pit lane has a row of garages, where cars stop for refuelling or repairs during a race.

Power unit

The integrated engine, motor and turbocharger of the new F1 car.

Roll cage

A strong frame that surrounds the cockpit of some racing cars, and protects the driver if the car rolls over.

Speedway

A road or track for motor racing. In North America, large oval speedways are used for superfast races.

Suspension

A system of springs and shock absorbers that makes the ride smoother as the wheels pass over bumps in the road or as a car takes corners.

Transmission

The system of gears that carries the power of the engine to the wheels. The power may be transferred only to the rear wheels, only to the front wheels, or to all four wheels.

Turbocharger

A mechanism that uses the flow of exhaust fumes to produce energy that is used to squash the air inside the engine. This gives the engine more power.

Wing

A bar at the back or front of a car that produces downforce to help the car to grip the road.

www.formula1.com
The official website of Formula 1, with race reports, videos and profiles of the teams and drivers.

www.indycar.com
Official website of the IndyCar Series. Results and upcoming races, plus all the facts and figures about the cars and drivers.

www.nascar.com
NASCAR's official website with information about the Sprint Cup, the Nationwide Series and the World Truck Series.

www.fia.com
Website of the International Automobile Federation (the FIA), the governing body of world motor sports, with features on Formula 1, endurance racing, touring car racing and rallying.

www.rallycrossrx.com
Coverage of the World Rallycross Championship, with photos, highlights of races and features on each driver.

www.btccpages.com
Website of the British Touring Car Championship, with the latest news and information.

www.24h-lemans.com/en/
Official website of the 24 Hours of Le Mans endurance race.

INDEX